GLOBAL CULTURES

Indian Culture

Anita Ganeri

Chicago, Illinois

www.capstonepub.com
Visit our website to find out more information about Heinemann-Raintree books.

To order:
☎ Phone 800-747-4992
🖥 Visit www.capstonepub.com
to browse our catalog and order online.

Edited by Charlotte Guillain, Abby Colich, and Vaarunika Dharmapala
Designed by Steve Mead
Original illustrations © Capstone Global Library Ltd 2013
Illustrations by Oxford Designers & Illustrators
Picture research by Ruth Blair

Originated by Capstone Global Library Ltd
Printed and bound in the United States of America in North Mankato, Minnesota.
022014   007974RP

16 15 14
10 9 8 7 6 5 4

Library of Congress Cataloging-in-Publication Data
Ganeri, Anita.
  Indian culture / Anita Ganeri.—1st ed.
    p. cm.—(Global cultures)
  Includes bibliographical references and index.
  ISBN 978-1-4329-6778-9 (hb)—ISBN 978-1-4329-6787-1 (pb) 1. Culture—History.
2. India—Social life and customs. 3. India—Civilization. I. Title.
  HM621.G326 2013
  306.0954—dc23   2011037702

Acknowledgments
We would like to thank the following for permission to reproduce photographs: Alamy pp. 16 (© Ladi Kirn), 20 (© Nikreates), 25 (© Dinodia Photos), 33 (© Dinodia Photos), 34 (© Rick Strange), 38 (© Hemis), 39 (© Friedrich Stark); Corbis pp. 8 (© Frederic Soltan), 13 (© Mohsin Raza/Reuters), 17 (© Earl & Nazima Kowall), 18 (© Phillipe Lissac/Godong), 19 (© Sanjeev Gupta/EPA), 21 (© Sheldan Collins), 23 (© David Cumming/Eye Ubiquitous), 28 (© Isabelle Vayron/Sygma), 29 (© EPA/Raminder Pal Singh), 30 (© Tibor Bognar), 37 (© Radius Images); Getty Images p. 14 (K. Asif/India Today Group); Photolibrary pp. 15 (Dinodia/Sinopictures); Photoshot pp. 10, 41 (© WpN), 11 (© EPA), 27 (© World Pictures), 31, 35 (© World Pictures); Shutterstock pp. 5 (© Pborowka), 7 (© VLADJ55), 9 (© Boris Stroujko), 22 (© Dmitri Mikitenko), 24 (© Jeremy Richards), 26 (© Claudine Van Massenhove), 43 top left (© Boris Stroujko), 43 top right (© Rafal Cichawa), 43 bottom left (© Jeremy Richards), 43 bottom right (© Aleynikov Pavel), design features (© Brandon Bourdages).

Cover photograph of a smiling Indian girl reproduced with permission of Corbis (© Blaine Harrington III). Cover design feature of a colorful textile reproduced with permission of Shutterstock (© Brandon Bourdages).

CONTENTS

Some words are shown in bold, **like this**. You can find out what they mean by looking in the glossary.

INTRODUCING INDIAN CULTURE

What do you imagine when you think of Indian **culture**? What sights and sounds come into your mind? Do you see beautiful temples and palaces? Or do you think of Indian food and fabulous silk **saris**?

India is located in South Asia. On the western side is the Arabian Sea. On the eastern side is the Bay of Bengal. To the north are the Himalayas, the world's highest mountains. India is the world's seventh biggest country. It is about one-third the size of the United States. It is home to more than a billion people—about one-seventh of all the people on Earth.

India is an ancient country with a long history. Over the last 5,000 years, it has been invaded many times. Each time, the people who came to India from other countries brought their own customs and traditions, which have left their mark on Indian culture.

What is culture?

Culture includes the values, beliefs, and attitudes of a place. It is about how people live and worship and about the music, art, and literature they produce. Because of its huge size and long history, Indian culture is incredibly varied. There are many different groups of people in India eating different foods, following different beliefs, speaking different languages, and wearing different clothes. However, they also have many things in common. For example, people all over India are fans of the sport **cricket** and love going to the movies.

BELIEFS AND FESTIVALS

Religion is very important in Indian culture and in people's lives there. It can determine where and how people live, whom they marry, what food they eat, and how they dress.

More than 80 percent of Indians are **Hindus**, and about 13 percent are **Muslims**. There are smaller numbers of **Christians**, **Sikhs**, **Buddhists**, and **Jains**.

Hinduism

Hindus follow the religion of Hinduism, which goes back at least 4,000 years. Hindus have many different beliefs and ways of worshiping. Most Hindus believe in a great spirit called Brahman. Some Hindus call Brahman "God." They also believe in many **deities** who represent Brahman's different qualities and powers.

The Buddha

The Buddha was a royal prince who was born in northeast India (modern-day Nepal) in about 563 BCE. He was named Siddhattha Gotama and grew up in great luxury. Despite this, he decided to live as a poor, wandering monk. He wanted to find a way for people to live happier lives.

After many years of **meditation**, Gotama became the Buddha, which means "the **enlightened** one." Today, there are very few Buddhists in India, but Buddhism has spread to other parts of Asia and around the world.

This is the colorful tower of a Hindu temple. It is decorated with carvings of gods and goddesses.

Did you know?

Below is a prayer to Lord Ganesh, the elephant-headed deity. Hindus believe that Ganesh removes obstacles. They pray to him before starting *puja* or doing any new or important task, such as going on a journey or moving.

"O Lord Ganesh, with
    curved trunk
And large body,
Shining with the brilliance
Of a thousand suns.
Take away all obstacles
From my good actions."

Hindu worship

Many Hindus visit the **mandir** (temple) to worship. They take part in **puja** (worship), saying prayers, singing songs, and making offerings of fruit, rice, flowers, and money to a **murti** (sacred image), in return for a blessing. Hindus believe that the *mandir* is Brahman's home on Earth. Each *mandir* is dedicated to a different deity or holy person, and a *murti* of that deity stands in the *mandir*. Hindus believe that Brahman is present in the *murti*. Through the *murti*, Brahman accepts the worshipers' love and devotion. Most Hindus also have a small **shrine** or a shrine room at home.

These Hindus are worshiping *murtis* in a temple.

Sikh worship

Sikhs follow the religion of Sikhism, which began in northwest India about 500 years ago. It was introduced by a holy man, named Nanak, who taught that everyone is equal and should be respected. Nanak became the first Sikh *Guru* (teacher). Sikhs worship in a building called a *gurdwara*, which means "door of the Guru." Any place can be a *gurdwara* as long as it has a copy of the **Guru Granth Sahib**, the Sikhs' holy book.

The Golden Temple in Amritsar is the holiest site in Sikhism. This stunning *gurdwara* was completed in 1604.

Hindu festivals

There are Hindu festivals throughout the year celebrating the seasons, stories of the deities, or family events. Some are small, local festivals held in homes or villages. Others are celebrated all across India.

The most important festival is Diwali, the festival of lights, which falls in October or November. People light small lamps, called *divas*, and place them by their doors and windows to guide the god, Lord Rama, back home after his long exile. The *divas* are also meant to welcome Lakshmi, the goddess of wealth and good fortune, into people's homes.

At Diwali, Hindus light candles, set off fireworks, and give each other gifts of jewelry and new clothes.

Festival of spring

Holi is a lively and colorful festival held in February or March. Traditionally, it was when farmers in India brought in the first wheat harvest of the year. It is a time for the whole family to have fun. Children shower each other with colored powder and squirt colored water from pumps and water pistols. Later, people visit friends and family with gifts of sweet treats to continue the celebrations.

The custom of throwing colored water at Holi is a reminder of a story about the god Lord Krishna. He was famous for making mischief and playing tricks on his friends.

YOUNG PEOPLE

The festival of Raksha Bandhan is a special time for brothers and sisters. After prayers, a girl ties a colorful bracelet, called a *rakhi*, around her brother's right wrist to protect him from evil. In return, he gives his sister a gift and promises to look after her in the coming year.

Sikh festivals

Festivals are important in other Indian religions, too. In April, Sikhs celebrate the festival of Baisakhi. The festival remembers the founding of the *Khalsa* (Sikh community) by Guru Gobind Singh in 1699. At Baisakhi, there are services in the *gurdwara* and a nonstop reading of the Guru Granth Sahib. It is also the time when Sikhs take down the special flag flying outside their *gurdwara*. They clean the flagpole, replace its cloth cover, and put up a new flag. The flag is called the *Nishan Sahib*, or "respected flag."

Guru Gobind Singh (1666–1708)

Guru Gobind Singh became the tenth Sikh Guru when he was only nine years old. A brilliant scholar and brave warrior, he fought many battles to protect the Sikh religion. He did not name a human Guru to lead the Sikhs after him. Just before his death, he told the Sikhs that their holy book, the Guru Granth Sahib, would be their leader and teacher.

Muslim festivals

The two most important festivals in Islam are 'Id-ul-Fitr and 'Id-ul-Adha. The word 'Id means "celebration." 'Id-ul-Fitr marks the breaking of the **fast** at the end of **Ramadan**. The day begins with prayers when people thank Allah. Later, families celebrate with parties, gifts, and a feast. 'Id-ul-Adha takes place at the end of the month in which many Muslims make the **Hajj pilgrimage**. At this time, people remember the story of the Prophet Ibrahim and his love for Allah. A sheep or goat is killed for a special feast.

This Sikh man is dressed to celebrate the festival of Baisakhi.

FAMILY AND SOCIETY

Indian society is quite traditional, although life for some people is changing fast. About two-thirds of Indians still live in villages, which are scattered throughout the countryside. There are estimated to be about 600,000 villages.

Village life

Villagers are often farmers, growing crops or raising animals on small plots of land that they rent from a landlord. Most are very poor and live in small, simple houses. The village may also have a *mandir* or a **mosque** and a small school. Some villages are still governed by a *panchayat*, a group of elected elders. The *panchayat* hears villagers' complaints and deals with any problems they may have.

This *panchayat* is discussing important village matters.

City life

India has some of the most crowded cities in the world. The largest are New Delhi (which has around 21 million people) and Mumbai (which has around 19 million people). City populations are growing fast, as poor people from the countryside move into cities in search of work and a better life. Indian cities are full of contrasts, with modern skyscrapers and office blocks standing side-by-side with sprawling **slums**.

Mumbai is the commercial capital of India.

Did you know?

India has 22 official languages. There are also hundreds of local languages. Hindi is spoken by more than 40 percent of people, making it the fifth most spoken language in the world. India used to be ruled by Great Britain, and English is still spoken across the country.

Family life

Family life is very important in Indian culture. Many Hindus live in large families, with children, parents, grandparents, aunts, uncles, and cousins all together under one roof. This is called a joint family. The eldest man is considered to be the head of the family. Everyone shares in the family duties and takes care of each other. Traditionally, newly married women go to live with their husband's family.

YOUNG PEOPLE

From a very early age, Hindu children are taught to love and respect their elders. Traditionally, they greet their parents, grandparents, aunts, and uncles by bowing and touching their feet. This is meant as a sign of respect. In return, their elders touch the children's heads to give them their blessing.

While many people in India still live in joint families, some people are now choosing to live apart.

A Hindu wedding

Traditionally, Hindu weddings are often arranged by a couple's family. This custom is still strong, but many couples are now allowed a say in their parents' choice of partner and can refuse if they want to. The wedding itself lasts for several days, with many different rituals for the bride and groom to complete. These include walking around the sacred fire and taking seven steps together. At each step, the couple makes a vow to each other for good health, wealth, and happiness. Hindu brides traditionally wear red saris, with beautiful jewelry and makeup. After the ceremony, there is a feast.

This Hindu bride and groom are taking seven steps around the sacred fire.

A new baby

Special ceremonies, or *samskaras*, mark important times in a Hindu's life. When a baby is about 12 days old, there is a naming ceremony at home or in the *mandir*. The priest draws up the baby's **horoscope** to see what the future holds. He also says prayers, asking for the gods' blessings on the baby.

Then the priest chooses a letter of the alphabet, based on the baby's time and place of birth. The baby's name should start with this letter. The father whispers the name in the baby's ear. Many Hindu children are named after gods and goddesses or have names with other religious meanings.

This Hindu baby is at her naming ceremony. The mark on her forehead is a sign of blessing.

Sacred thread

When some Hindu boys are about 10 years old, another very important *samskara* takes place. This is called the sacred thread ceremony. It marks the beginning of the boy's adult life. During the ceremony, the priest drapes a long loop of thread over the boy's left shoulder and under his right arm. Then he whispers a prayer, called the *Gayatri Mantra*, into the boy's ear. The boy learns this prayer and, from then on, recites it every day. Girls do not have a sacred thread ceremony.

This group of boys is attending a sacred thread ceremony.

Did you know?

When a Hindu dies, the body is **cremated** while a priest chants prayers. Later, the ashes are scattered, ideally in the sacred Ganges River. Ten days of mourning follow. After that, Hindus believe, the person's soul is **reincarnated** in another body.

ART AND ARCHITECTURE

Since ancient times, Indian artists have created beautiful paintings, carvings, and sculptures. Much of this art has been inspired by religion and has been used to decorate temples and other holy places. Indian art has also been influenced by the styles of artists who arrived from other places, such as Greece, Central Asia, and Europe.

Cave paintings

The Ajanta caves in western India were carved into a mountain around 1,500 to 2,000 years ago. Buddhist monks used them as places of worship. Inside many of the caves, artists have painted murals (paintings) on the walls. The murals show scenes from the *Jatakas*, a collection of stories about the Buddha's life. The caves were abandoned in 650 CE. They were rediscovered by a British army officer over 1,000 years later.

This mural in a cave at Ajanta shows a scene from one of the Buddha's past lives.

Miniature painting

The Mughals were Muslims from Central Asia who ruled large parts of India from the 1500s to the 1800s. Several Mughal emperors were great supporters of art, especially the miniature style of painting, where pictures are painted on a small scale. Many of these highly detailed paintings showed scenes of life at court or wildlife.

Many artists were influenced by the Mughal style. This miniature shows the Hindu god, Krishna, and his companion, Radha. It dates from the mid-1700s.

M. F. Husain (1915–2011)

M. F. Husain was a famous modern Indian artist. As a boy, he sold his school books to buy paints and brushes. To earn a living, he later painted billboards that advertised movies. Among his favorite subjects were scenes from Indian street life.

Sculpture

Indian sculptors are highly skilled craftspeople, producing fine carvings and sculptures in stone, wood, and bronze. Like paintings, many of these works of art have religious themes and decorate temples and other places of worship.

The sculptors who make Hindu *murtis* (see page 8) follow strict rules set out in the ancient sacred texts. These give instructions about the exact proportions, materials, and techniques the sculptors should use in their work. Each part of an image tells a story or has a special meaning. For example, Hindu deities are often shown with several heads or arms, which represent their special characteristics or powers.

This is a bronze figure of Krishna, one of the most popular Hindu gods. He is often shown as a young man playing a flute.

Images of the Buddha

In the earliest works of Buddhist art, the Buddha was never shown in person. Instead, he was shown by symbols, such as footprints, a wheel, a lotus flower, and a horse. Each symbol had a special meaning in the Buddha's life. Later, statues of the Buddha began to be made. They showed different signs that marked the Buddha as an extraordinary person. For example, long earlobes showed that he came from a noble family, and tightly curled hair showed that he was a very holy man.

This huge statue of the Buddha is in Bodh Gaya in India. This is the place where the Buddha gained enlightenment, and it is a sacred site for Buddhists.

Textiles

Indian textiles are famous around the world. Each region has its own fabrics and designs. For example, Rajasthan in western India is famous for its mirror work in which tiny, round mirrors are sewn into cloth.

Textiles range from simple cotton cloth to richly **embroidered** silks used for making saris. Saris are worn by many Indian women and are made from long pieces of cloth, usually 18 feet (5.5 meters) long. Some of the most famous silk saris come from the city of Varanasi in northern India. They are made from heavy silk, woven with beautiful gold or silver thread.

Saris are often highly decorated.

Manish Malhotra (born 1965)

Manish Malhotra is one of India's leading fashion designers. He began his career making elaborate costumes for **Bollywood** movie stars. Then, in 1998, he held his first mainstream fashion show. His collections of clothes mix traditional Indian textiles, colors, and embroidery with modern fabrics and designs.

Jewelry

Indian jewelry is not just for decoration. It also has a special meaning. Gold and silver are symbols of the sun and the moon, and each type of gemstone is associated with a deity.

On her wedding day, a Hindu bride wears lots of heavy jewelry. Once she is married, she wears a necklace called a *mangala sutra*. It is a gold pendant worn on a black and gold beaded chain. It is a symbol of her marriage, just as a wedding ring is in many cultures.

This is just some of the elaborate jewelry a Hindu bride will wear on her wedding day. She will also wear earrings, necklaces, and a nose ring.

Architecture

There are amazing buildings all over India. Like other Indian art forms, architecture is often linked to religion, and it has been greatly influenced by outside cultures and styles.

The most famous building in India, the Taj Mahal, was commissioned by the Mughal Emperor, Shah Jahan, as a tomb for his wife, Mumtaz Mahal. Building began in 1632 and took about 20 years. The Taj Mahal is designed in a Persian style used for tombs and mosques. It is built from white marble, topped by a huge dome. Images of people or animals are forbidden in Islam, so the building was decorated with verses from the **Qur'an**, the Muslim holy book, as well as patterns, flowers, and semiprecious stones.

This is a decorated archway inside the Taj Mahal. Look closely and you can see exquisite carvings and patterns.

British buildings

From 1784 to 1947, India came under British rule. In 1911 the British moved the capital from Kolkata to New Delhi, a city planned by British architects. One of the new buildings was the enormous Rashtrapati Bhavan. Its design is a mixture of European and Indian styles, with *chattris* (domes), *jalis* (stone grilles), and carvings of cobras, elephants, and temple bells.

Rashtrapati Bhavan is now the official residence of the president.

Did you know?

Legend says that Shah Jahan wanted to build a black marble copy of the Taj Mahal on the opposite bank of the river. This was intended to be his own tomb. He was overthrown and imprisoned by his son, Aurangzeb, before he could put his plan into action.

PERFORMANCE

Music plays an important part in Indian culture. Stories from the Hindu sacred texts are often set to music, and religious songs, called *bhajans*, are sung in the *mandir*.

Classical music

Classical Indian music dates back thousands of years. It is performed by a group of musicians. They play instruments including the *sitar* (played like a guitar), the *tablas* (drums), and the *sarangi* (played with a bow, like a cello). They do not follow a set piece of music. The music is based on sets of notes, called *ragas*. Each *raga* suggests a different mood—for example, love or sadness and time of day. The musicians make up the rest of the music around the *raga*. *Ragas* can also be sung on their own or to music.

These musicians are playing (from left to right) a *sitar*, *tablas*, and a harmonium in the courtyard of a *mandir*.

Bhangra beat

Each region of India has its own folk music and songs. *Bhangra* is a lively form of music from the Punjab in northwestern India. It was originally played to celebrate the harvest. A large drum, called a *dhol*, beats out a strong rhythm for dancing. *Bhangra* has been mixed with other types of music, such as hip-hop and reggae, to also become a popular modern form of music.

These *bhangra* dance moves are based on the way farmers work their land.

Did you know?

The most popular type of music in India is *filmi*, the songs sung in Bollywood movies. The songs are catchy and lively, mixing classical and popular music. They are usually recorded by professional singers, then lip-synched to by the actors and actresses.

Dance

There are also many different styles of Indian dance. Folk dances are often performed at regional festivals, while every Bollywood movie features several large-scale dances. Classical Indian dance is an ancient and dramatic form of dance that tells stories about the Hindu gods and goddesses.

Bharat natyam is a very graceful style of classical dance that began in southern India around 2,000 years ago. Female dancers use special eye and neck movements, rhythmical footwork, and hand gestures to tell a story. Each gesture can show a word or emotion, and the audience can follow the story from the dancer's hands alone. Dancers have to learn hundreds of these gestures and other body movements.

This *bharat natyam* dancer is telling a story with her movements alone.

Kathakali dance also began in southern India. It is a dramatic style of dancing, performed only by men. Dancers wear amazing costumes and makeup that give clues about the characters they play. Heroes or gods have green faces, demons have black faces, and women or holy men have yellow faces.

YOUNG PEOPLE

It takes years of training at a dance school to become a *kathakali* dancer. Students must gain a good knowledge of religious texts, music, and drama. They must also build up their physical stamina and flexibility, since performances are often very long. Toughest of all is learning to control their eye movements. These are very important in *kathakali*.

It takes eight or more hours for a *kathakali* dancer to apply his makeup.

Movies

The most popular form of entertainment in India is movies. About 14 million Indians watch Bollywood movies every day. "Bollywood" is the nickname given to India's enormous movie industry, based in the city of Mumbai (previously called Bombay). About 700 to 800 movies are made in Bollywood each year, mostly in the Hindi language.

Bollywood movies

Bollywood movies are usually blockbusters, with glamorous stars, catchy songs, dancing, action, romance, and comedy. They are known as *masala* movies, after the Indian spice mix, and aim to appeal to as many people as possible. They are usually around three hours long. *Filmi* music (see page 29) is often released before the movie itself to help pull audiences in. Popular actors can become superstars. Many use their fame to later take up careers in politics.

Some Bollywood movies have gone on to worldwide fame. Set during the time of British rule, *Lagaan* (2001) is the story of a cricket match between a team of poor villagers and a team of British officers. It won many awards and was nominated for an Oscar.

Amitabh Bacchan (born 1942)

One of the most famous Bollywood actors ever, Bacchan was the son of a Hindi poet and rose to fame in the 1970s. He has appeared in more than 150 movies and has also worked as a producer and television host. His son, Abhishek, is also a movie star.

Huge billboards advertising movies line the streets of Indian cities. These used to be painted by hand, but they are now mostly created on computers.

DAILY LIFE

Food plays a very important role in Indian culture. Like everything else in India, it varies greatly from place to place. Each region has its own cooking style, which is influenced by the terrain, climate, and crops. For example, *chapattis* and other types of Indian bread are eaten in northern India, where wheat grows well. More rice is eaten in the south, where it is widely grown. Spices, such as chilis, cardamom, turmeric, and cumin, are important in Indian cooking. Each region or even family has its own special spice mix, called *garam masala*.

This lush green field in southern India is planted with rice.

Food and religion

In India, religious beliefs often decide what people can and cannot eat. Most Hindus are vegetarians, which means they do not eat meat. They believe that it is important to respect all living things and so do not harm or kill animals. Some Hindus eat chicken or fish, but they will not eat beef. They believe that cows are sacred animals because they provide milk. Like Hindus, Sikhs are also traditionally vegetarian. Muslims do eat some meat, but it must be *halal* (food that is allowed). Pork is *haram* (food that is forbidden by the Qur'an).

Did you know?

Indian *mithai* (sweet treats) are made from milk, coconut, nuts, sugar, *ghee* (a type of butter), and cream cheese. People make them at home or buy them from bakeries. *Mithai* are given as gifts on special occasions. Popular *mithai* include *laddu* (balls of flour dipped in sugar syrup) and *barfi* (solidified squares of condensed milk cooked with sugar).

Eating

Each region of India has its own distinctive cooking style. In southern India, *idlis* and *dosas* are staple foods. *Idlis* are small, steamed rice cakes eaten with coconut chutney. *Dosas* are crispy rice pancakes, often filled with spicy vegetables. In northwest India, meat, such as chicken or lamb, is cooked in a *tandoor* (clay oven). This is called tandoori cooking, and it was introduced to India by the Mughals.

Food etiquette

Traditionally, Indians do not use cutlery to eat their food. They use the fingers of their right hands instead (their left hands are considered unclean). They scoop up food with a piece of bread or mix it with some rice. It is said that eating with your hands helps you avoid eating food that is too hot. Today, some Indians do use knives and forks, but many think that food tastes better when you eat it with your fingers.

YOUNG PEOPLE

In big Indian cities, Western-style fast food restaurants are becoming very popular among young people. The restaurants have adapted their menus to suit Indian tastes. For example, burgers are made with lamb or chicken, instead of beef. Pizzas come with extra chilis or with Indian toppings, such as tandoori chicken or *paneer* (curd cheese). There is also a wide range of vegetarian options.

A traditional Indian meal is served on a large, metal plate, called a *thali*, with small bowls of vegetables, *dal* (lentils), and *dahi* (yogurt). There are also rice or bread, pickles, and *papadum* (flatbread). In southern India, a large banana leaf may be used instead of a *thali*.

Leisure

In their leisure time, Indians enjoy taking part in and watching a variety of sports and games. Kite flying is very popular, both for fun and as part of festivals, such as Makar Sankranti. This is a spring festival held in January. At this time, people take part in kite-fighting competitions, using their kite lines to try to bring other kites down.

Kabaddi is a fast-paced game played by two teams. Each team takes turns in sending a "raider" into the opponent's half of the field. The raider tries to win points by tagging members of the other team. All the time, he has to hold his breath and chant the word *kabaddi*. Meanwhile, the other team tries to stop him from reaching home base.

During competitions, people fly their kites from rooftops.

These Indian boys are playing cricket in the street.

Crazy for cricket

India's most popular sport by far is cricket. People play in the streets, in parks, or on beaches—wherever they can find an open space. Cricket fever is particularly strong when international cricket teams visit India to play matches. Members of the Indian cricket team are national heroes, and the team won the cricket World Cup in 2011.

Sachin Tendulkar (born 1973)

Sachin Tendulkar is one of the world's greatest cricket players. Born in Mumbai, he began his cricket career in high school. A master batter, he has set many records in the sport. He is a major sports hero to people young and old across India—and across the world.

INDIAN CULTURE IN THE 21ST CENTURY

All over India, people still follow traditional customs and lifestyles, as their families have done for centuries. However, India is also changing at a rapid pace.

Over the last few years, many international companies have set up offices in India, taking advantage of its highly skilled workforce. This has led to many cultural changes, including a rise in the number of people with good jobs and money to spend. More people can afford to buy their own homes, so many are moving away from their joint families and setting out on their own. In the big cities where they work, Western-style supermarkets and coffee shops are taking the place of traditional markets and snack stalls.

YOUNG PEOPLE

Children of Indians who have settled in other countries sometimes face cultural challenges. At home, they are often expected to follow their parents' or grandparents' culture. They may learn to speak an Indian language, wear Indian dress, and eat Indian food. At the same time, they must fit in with the culture of the Western country they live in.

These young people are visiting a Western-style shopping center in the city of Bangalore.

Indian culture has also had a huge impact on other parts of the world where Indians have settled, such as the United States, Canada, and the United Kingdom. Indian communities in these countries have established their own *mandirs* and mosques, fabric and food stores, and restaurants.

Indian culture remains a mixture of the traditional and the modern. It continues to change and adapt to outside influences, as it has done for thousands of years and will continue to do for many years ahead.

TIMELINE

BCE

1500   Aryans from Central Asia invade India. Their religion forms the basis of Hinduism. The origins of Indian classical music can also be found in Aryan culture.

563   The Buddha (founder of Buddhism) is born

CE

about 4   The *bharat natyam* dance is first performed in southern India

1001   Muslims from Afghanistan invade northwest India

1469   Guru Nanak (the founder of Sikhism) is born

1526   The Mughal Empire is founded

1600s   *Kathakali* dance is first performed in southern India

1632   Shah Jahan begins building the Taj Mahal

1699   Guru Gobind Singh founds the Sikh *Khalsa*

1784   The British take political control of India

1911   The capital of India is moved from Kolkata to New Delhi

1931   The first Hindi movie with sound is made (*Alam Ara*)

1942   The movie star Amitabh Bacchan is born

1947   India gains independence from Britain

1950s   Many Indians begin to leave to settle in other countries

1973   Cricket player Sachin Tendulkar is born

2000   India marks the birth of its billionth citizen

2011   The artist M. F. Husain dies

2011   India wins the Cricket World Cup

CULTURAL MAP

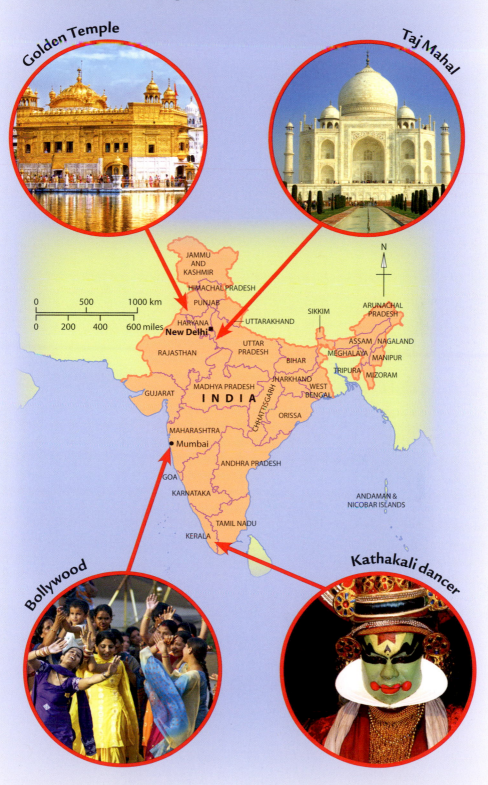

Golden Temple

Taj Mahal

N

JAMMU AND KASHMIR

HIMACHAL PRADESH

PUNJAB

| 0 | 500 | 1000 km |

| 0 | 200 | 400 | 600 miles |

HARYANA

New Delhi

UTTARAKHAND

SIKKIM

ARUNACHAL PRADESH

RAJASTHAN

UTTAR PRADESH

BIHAR

ASSAM   NAGALAND

MEGHALAYA   MANIPUR

TRIPURA   MIZORAM

GUJARAT

MADHYA PRADESH

JHARKHAND

CHHATTISGARH

WEST BENGAL

I N D I A

ORISSA

MAHARASHTRA

• Mumbai

GOA

ANDHRA PRADESH

KARNATAKA

ANDAMAN & NICOBAR ISLANDS

TAMIL NADU

KERALA

Bollywood

Kathakali dancer

GLOSSARY

Bollywood Indian movie industry, based in Mumbai (formerly known as Bombay)

Buddhist person who follows the religion of Buddhism, which began in India in the 400s BCE

Christian person who follows the religion of Christianity, which began in the Middle East about 2,000 years ago

cremate when the body of a dead person is burned to ashes

cricket sport that involves hitting a ball with a bat. Two teams with 11 players each compete on a field with two markers called wickets. It is similar in some ways to baseball.

culture customs, social organization, and achievements of a particular nation, people, or group

deity god or goddess

embroidery art of sewing designs on cloth

enlightened when someone has understood the truth

fast go without food or drink for a certain length of time

Guru Granth Sahib holy book of the Sikhs

Hajj pilgrimage to Makkah (the sacred city of the Muslims) that all Muslims try to make at least once in their lives

Hindu person who follows the religion of Hinduism, which began in India at least 4,000 years ago

horoscope chart showing the position of the stars and planets at the time of a person's birth. Hindus use horoscopes to choose dates for weddings and other important events.

Jain person who follows the religion of Jainism, which began in India in the 400s BCE *mandir* place where Hindus may go to worship; also called a temple

meditation clearing the mind and controlling one's breathing

mosque building in which Muslims meet and worship

murti sacred image of a god or goddess

Muslim person who follows the religion of Islam, which began in Arabia in the 600s CE

pilgrimage journey to a holy place that is important in a religion

puja act of worship in Hinduism and Buddhism

Qur'an holy book of the Muslims

Ramadan month in the Muslim calendar when Muslims fast from sunrise to sunset every day

reincarnate to be born again. Hindus, Buddhists, and Sikhs believe that, when you die, you are born again in another body.

samskaras special ceremonies that mark important times in a Hindu's life

sari clothing worn by many Indian women. A sari is a long piece of fabric that is wrapped around the body.

shrine building or small structure that is devoted to a religion

Sikh person who follows the religion of Sikhism, which began in India about 500 years ago

slum overcrowded area in a city that is inhabited by very poor people

FIND OUT MORE

Books

Apte, Sunita. *India* (True Books: Countries). New York: Children's Press, 2009.

Brownlie Bojang, Ali. *India* (Countries Around the World). Chicago: Heinemann Library, 2012.

Ganeri, Anita. *India* (Countries in the News). North Mankato, Minn.: Smart Apple Media, 2008.

Ganeri, Anita. *India* (World of Food). Minneapolis: Clara House, 2010.

Ganeri, Anita. *Prayer and Worship* series. North Mankato, Minn.: Sea to Sea, 2008.

Websites

https://www.cia.gov/library/publications/the-world-factbook/geos/in.html
Find up-to-the-minute facts about India on this website.

india.gov.in
This website includes information about health, education, and culture in India. There is also a kids' corner to check out.

kids.nationalgeographic.com/kids/places/find/india/
Find out more about India's geography, history, people, and more at this website.

worldmusic.nationalgeographic.com/view/page.basic/country/content.country/india_31/en_US
Learn more about Indian music at this website and listen to recordings by different Indian musicians.

Places to visit

The Freer Gallery of Art and the Arthur M. Sackler Gallery,
Washington, D.C.
www.asia.si.edu
The Freer and Sackler Galleries focus on the art of Asia,
and their collection contains many important examples of
Indian art.

The Los Angeles County Museum of Art, California
www.lacma.org
The Los Angeles County Museum of Art has an impressive
collection of Indian art.

Metropolitan Museum of Art, New York City
www.metmuseum.org
The Metropolitan Museum of Art has galleries with objects
from India, including jewelry, paintings, and more.

More topics to research

What topic did you like reading about most in this book?
Did you find out anything that you thought was particularly
interesting? Choose a topic that you liked, such as food,
buildings, or religion, and try to find out more about it. You
could visit one of the places mentioned above, take a look at
one of the websites listed here, or visit your local library to do
some research. You could also try putting on a sari, watching a
Bollywood movie, or trying some Indian treats!

INDEX

GLOBAL CULTURES

Indian Culture

This beautifully illustrated series gives an introduction to some of the world's most fascinating and ancient cultures. Discover different cultures' approaches to visual arts and performance and find out about important beliefs, traditions, and customs. Find out about the role of family and community in these cultures and explore how cultures are changing and developing in the 21st century.

Each book contains chapters focusing on a different aspect of culture, with fact boxes providing more detailed information on life for young people and biographies of key figures. A timeline, a cultural map, and suggestions for further research are also included.

Titles in the series:
African Culture
American Indian Cultures
Chinese Culture
Indian Culture
Indigenous Australian Cultures
Islamic Culture
Japanese Culture
Mexican Culture

What happens in a *mandir*?

◆

What is a *samskara*?

◆

Who were the Mughals?

Author
Anita Ganeri was born in India and has an MA in Indian Studies from Cambridge University. She is an award-winning author of children's information books, including many on India and southern Asia.

Consultant
Lawrence Saez is a specialist in the political economy of South Asia. He teaches political science at the School of Oriental and African Studies (SOAS) in London. He is also the director of the Center for South Asian Studies at SOAS.

SOCIAL STUDIES · Level S

ISBN 978-1-4329-6787-1

9 781432 967871